Our Brother Has Down Syndrome

LaShanda Stringfield

SUSU Entertainment LLC
P.O. Box 1621
Cypress, Texas 77410
susuentertainmentllc@gmail.com

Printed in the United States of America

Name: LaShanda Stringfield, Author

Title: | Our Brother Has Down Syndrome

Summary: Mom and Dad were excited about welcoming their baby boy home after having four daughters. They didn't know that their bundle of joy would have challenges and be diagnosed with Down syndrome but with family support, kindness, patience and love they would conquer any obstacles along the way.

Identifiers:
ISBN: 978-1-956292-25-1 (Paperback)
ISBN: 978-1-956292-26-8 (Hardcover)

Subjects: | Down syndrome awareness | Family Support | Patience and Love

Book Cover Design © 2023 by SUSU Entertainment LLC

INTRODUCTION

The girls were excited about the new arrival of their baby brother. They were making plans to read, learn, play, and build a special bond together. After the joy of having four daughters, Mom and Dad were ready to welcome a son with open arms.

Little did they know, their pride and joy would come with some challenges that would require in-depth conversations with their daughters, but with love, patience, prayer, and family support, they would be able to conquer any obstacles they faced along the way.

The night before our baby brother was born, we sat around our mom in anticipation of finally having a brother. He will have four big sisters who will love and protect him.

Mom's water broke the next day and Daddy assisted her to the nearest hospital. Daddy was happy to welcome a new baby to the family.

Memaw stayed and helped us keep the house fresh and clean. Carissa started decorating for the arrival of their baby brother.

Our baby brother is here! Our baby brother is here!
The girls waved and clapped in excitement with Memaw as their Mom,
Dad, and baby brother arrived.

Our baby brother's name is Charles. Mom named him after her Dad. He is a beautiful baby. We enjoy taking turns holding him.

LaCoyia likes to give Charles sweet kisses. She explained to her sisters how you must always support a baby's head when holding them. London brought a blanket to cover her brother up. The girls loved their brother.

Carissa said proudly, "I think we should call him Bubby." Bubby smiled. "I think he likes his nickname."

Everyone was happy that the decorations for baby Charles's homecoming was complete. Blue, gold, and white balloons filled the family room. Candace started to clap until she realized that Charles had fallen asleep.

After their baby brother's nap, Mom and Dad asked everyone to gather in the living room. "We want to talk to you all about Bubby," they said.

We could tell from the look on their faces that it was very important.

Mom stated, "Your baby brother Charles has Down syndrome." "What does that mean Mom?" London asked.

Mom explained, "It is a condition where a child has an extra chromosome." Mom got out her chart and created a chromosome illustration.

"What are chromosomes?" Carissa asked. Dad explained, "Chromosomes are tiny packages of genes in the body that determines how a baby's body forms and functions as it grows during pregnancy and after birth."

"You're scaring us, Mom. Can we fix it?" LaCoyia asked.
"No, we can't fix it. What it means is that he won't be able to do certain things as soon as other children normally would, but with lots of love and support from our family, he'll get there." Mom added.

Mom and the girls went outside for some fresh air while Daddy watched Bubby. Mom clarified, "Some children with Down syndrome may experience intellectual and developmental disabilities or health issues. Some of Charles's issues may be mild, moderate, or severe."

London loved her baby brother Bubby so much but was sad to hear that he had Down syndrome. "Will he look like he is sick?" She asked.

"No, Bubby won't look sick but some of his features, like his eyes, face, and height may appear different and he may learn to sit up, crawl or walk slower than most children his age," Mom said.

"This is why God has blessed Charles with his strong sisters, you all will be able to help him," Dad stated.

"We will protect our baby brother from the bullies. The ones that like to pick on children that are different," Candace expressed. The sisters shook their heads in agreement.

"Unfortunately, some children can be mean, but we can help Charles make friends, encourage him to always speak up and build up his confidence to help protect him from any bullying behaviors." Mom expressed.

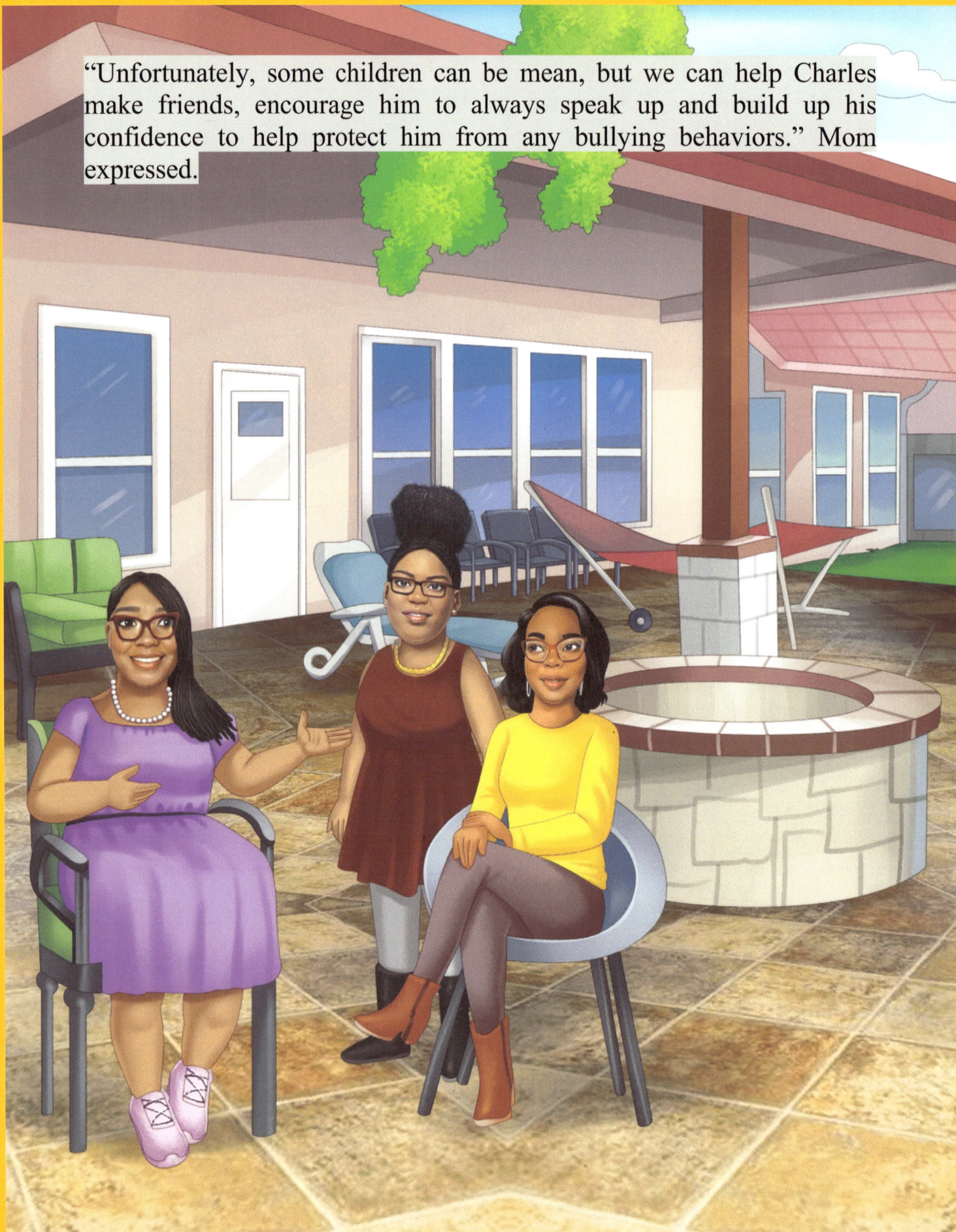

Candace went to sit with her Memaw on the swing to discuss the news they had gotten about Charles. Memaw explained, "Charles will not be defined by his diagnosis. He will be smart but will require us to have patience and understanding. He must also be taught when to hug someone and when he should keep an appropriate distance."

"Will he be able to play like normal children?" London asked. "Yes, he will be active, but he may require extra help in understanding how to play certain games." Mom answered.

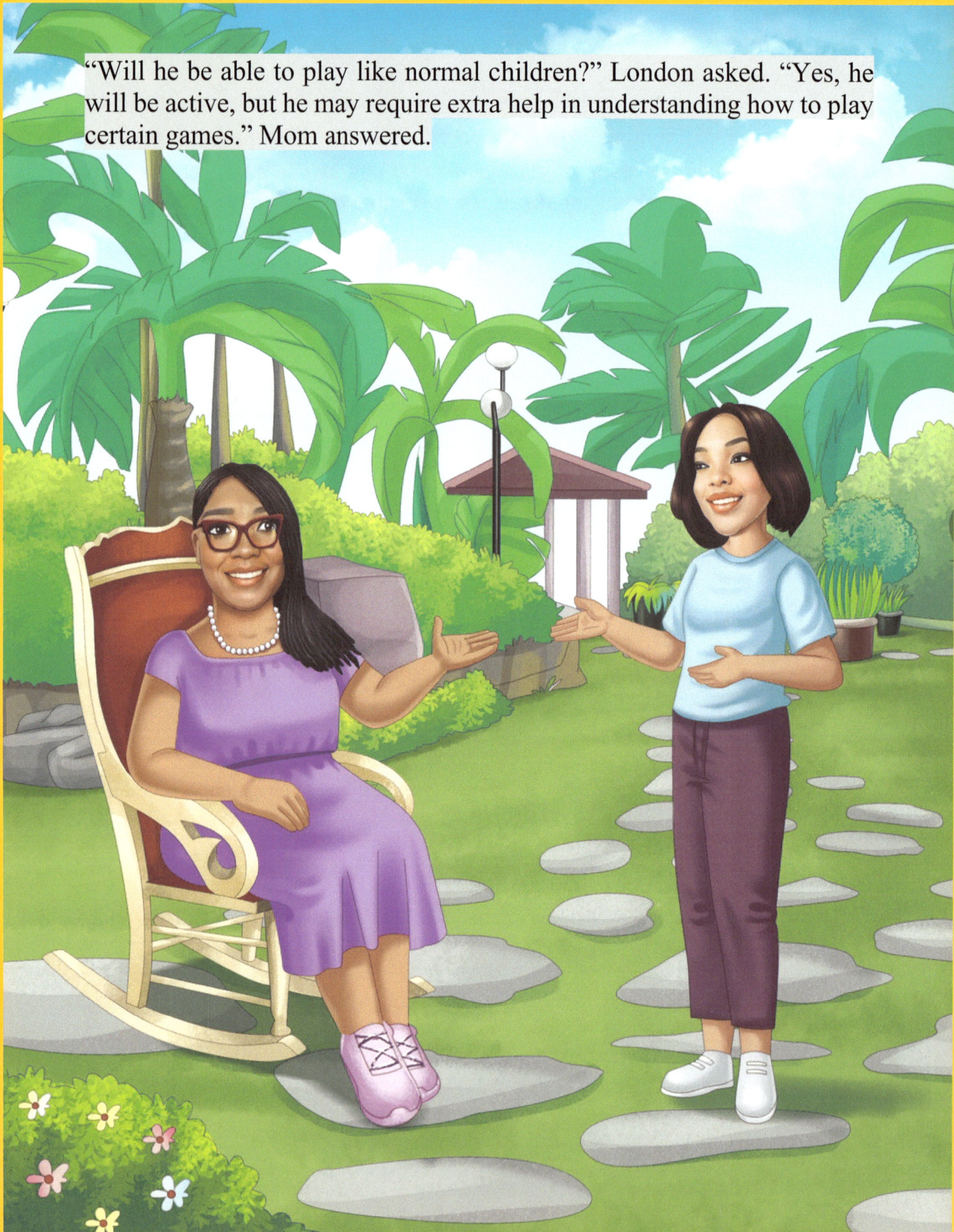

"Will Bubby have any friends?" LaCoyia asked. "Yes, he will have his family as his first friends, but he will meet a lot of friends in school and the community," Dad stated.

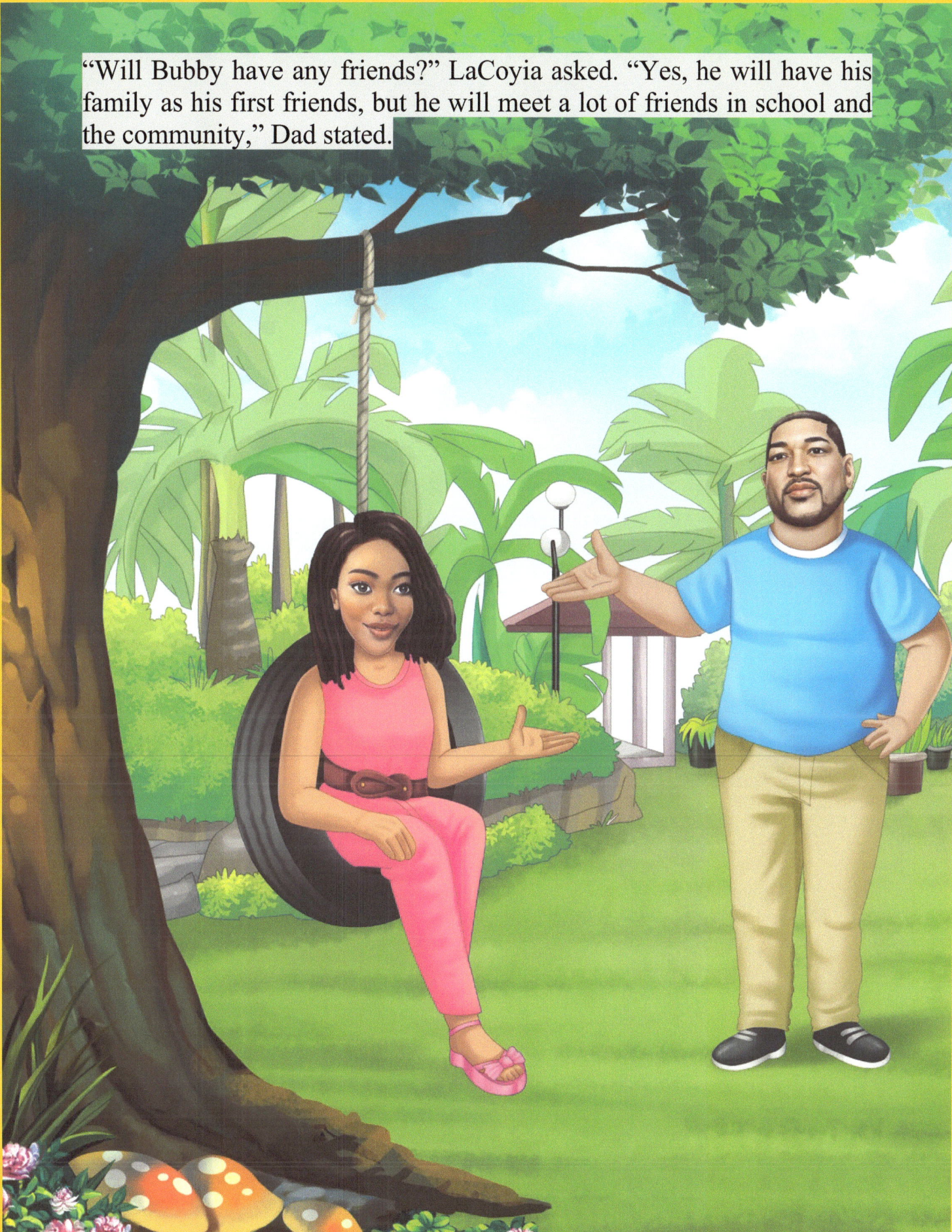

"How will we talk to Bubby?" The girls asked.

Daddy explained, "Communication may sometimes be challenging, but we must learn to always be loving and patient. We may interact with Bubby verbally, non-verbally and sometimes use hand gestures. We can enjoy reading together, playing together, and learning together. Most importantly, we will treat Charles like a child that doesn't have disabilities."

The girls noticed that Bubby was smiling in his sleep.

London perked up and said, "Wow! He is a healthy and happy baby!" Everyday Bubby was grinning and wiggling in his sister's arms. The girls felt proud of their baby brother.

"What will happen when Bubby gets older? Will he be able to work as an adult?" Carissa asked. "Yes, Bubby may have challenges but with hard work, great support and guidance, he will be successful wherever he may choose to work," Daddy expressed.

"There are also a lot of volunteer opportunities for young adults with Down syndrome that will help prepare them with lifelong support and the necessary skills needed to start working," Daddy added.

"I hope Bubby likes to eat sweets. Maybe we can bake cakes, cookies, cupcakes, and pies together," the girls added.

"I'm sure he will enjoy helping you all bake some sweet treats," Mom and Dad chuckled.

"Does Down syndrome hurt? Will our baby brother be in pain?" LaCoyia asked.

Daddy explained to the girls what it means for Charles to have Down syndrome. "No, he won't be in pain. Your brother will just need extra love and attention from his family…like this." Out of the blue, Daddy grabbed the girls and started giving them more hugs and tickles.

The girls' behavior quickly changed from sadness to excitement. Daddy loved his girls and knew what it took to put smiles back on their faces.

Daddy stated, "Children with Down syndrome may have physical and mental delays, but they can still live healthy and happy lives. Your brother Charles will be a light in this world."

Mom added, "As Bubby grows, he will start early intervention, such as therapy." "Why would he need therapy?" Candace asked.

"Therapy helps you to be happier and healthier. It helps with life-long coping skills, you understand and learn how to communicate with others better, and it helps your overall mood and well-being."

"Therapy is good for anyone that may be going through a hard time," Mom explained.

"Soon, people will come to our house to help Charles in a lot of ways to help him grow stronger." Mom expressed.

Memaw waited on the front porch for Granny to arrive to see her new grandson.

Granny arrived. She was incredibly happy to see her newest grandson, Charles. "Oh Carlos, my son, he looks just like you!" Granny exclaimed.

"Thank you, Momma. That's my big boy!" Carlos said proudly. "We are very thankful that God has blessed us with a healthy baby boy."

Charles had brought the family so much joy. The family stood together in unity for Charles. Daddy began to say a prayer for him. "God, we thank you for our son, brother and grandson, Charles. May you keep him safe and bless him all the days of his life. In Jesus name."

"Amen!" Everyone said in unison as they lifted their hands with gratitude.

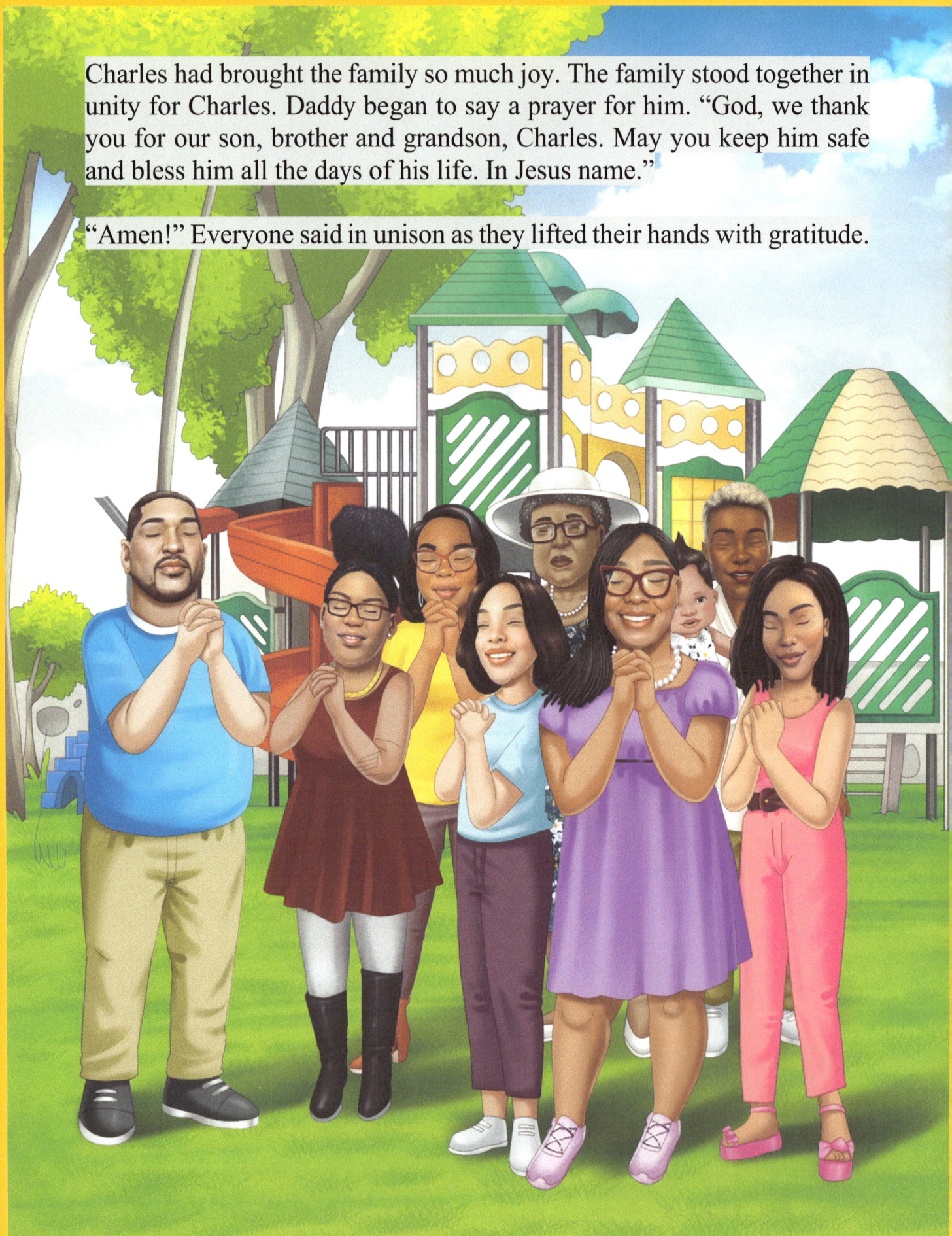

DEDICATION

We dedicate this book to our sweet, happy, playful, affectionate, sometimes mischievous, and loving son and brother Charles, better known as Bubby. You are a joy to our family with a heart of gold. Your love shines through for everyone who knows you to see. We are truly blessed to have you. We love you, Bubby!

Love,

Mommy, Sisters & Family

ACKNOWLEDGEMENTS

Thank you to my beautiful, loving and caring daughters, Carissa, LaCoyia, Candace and London. Your brother Charles is blessed to have four strong sisters that are loving, patient and kind.

Thank you to our brothers and sisters in Christ at the Eastside Church of Christ in Ocean Springs, MS.

Thank you to the faculty and staff at Magnolia Park Elementary School in Ocean Springs, MS and College Park Elementary School in Gautier, MS.

Thank you to all our family and friends that continue to provide unconditional love and support to my family. You all are greatly appreciated.

IN MEMORY OF

Carlos Stringfield

Charles Ard

ABOUT THE AUTHOR

LaShanda Stringfield lives in South Mississippi and enjoys every moment spent with her family. She is a lover of God, books and sweets. She began her love for reading when her mother read to her every night as a child. Her love for reading has led to a love for writing. This is her first book, and she plans to write many more.

Let's Connect

Email: lnstringfield@yahoo.com

Facebook: @bubbybooks21

Instagram: @bubbybooks21

For more information about Down syndrome, contact:

National Down Syndrome Society
1155 15th Street NW, Suite 540
Washington, DC 20005
Main: 1-800-221-4602
Direct: 202-751-6013
Email: info@ndss.org
Website: www.ndss.org

OTHER BOOKS FROM THE AUTHOR

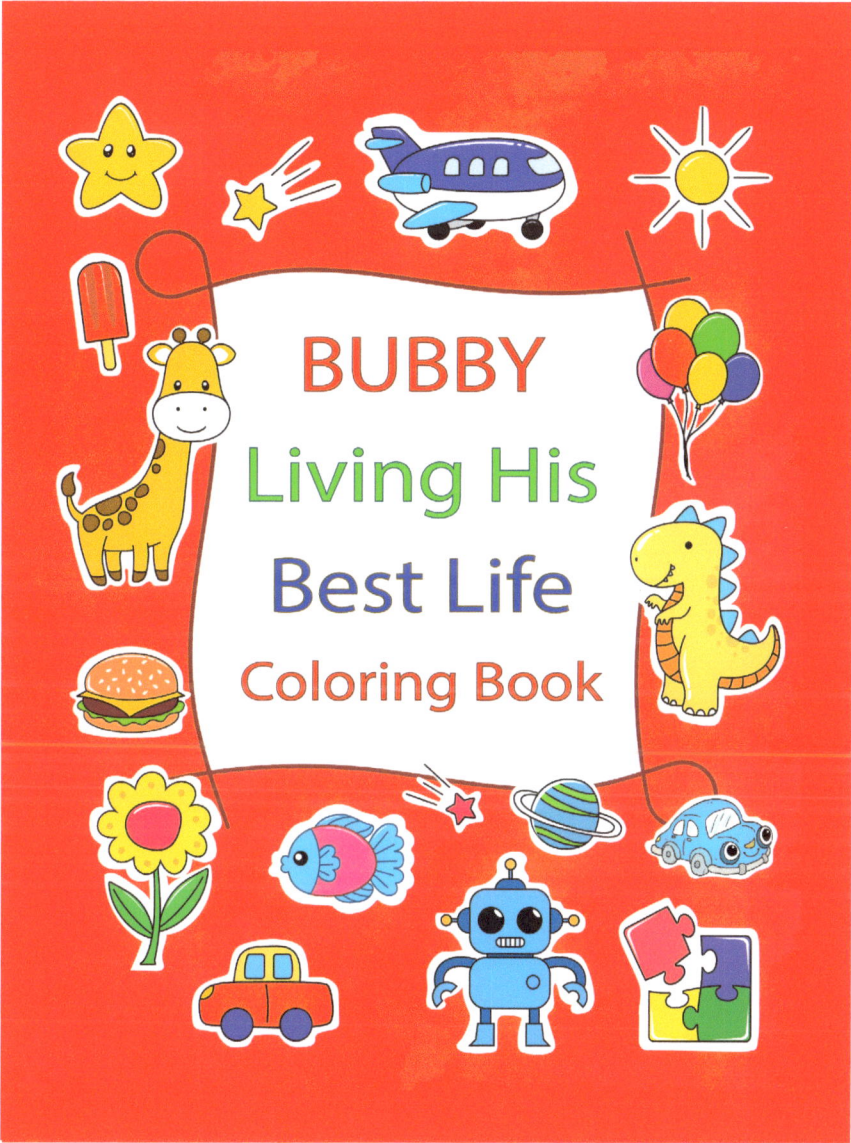

BUBBY
Living His
Best Life
Coloring Book

www.ingramcontent.com/pod-product-compliance
Lightning Source LLC
LaVergne TN
LVHW072055070426
835508LV00002B/107